Deer make homes in the forest.

Deer might sleep in tall grass or under trees.

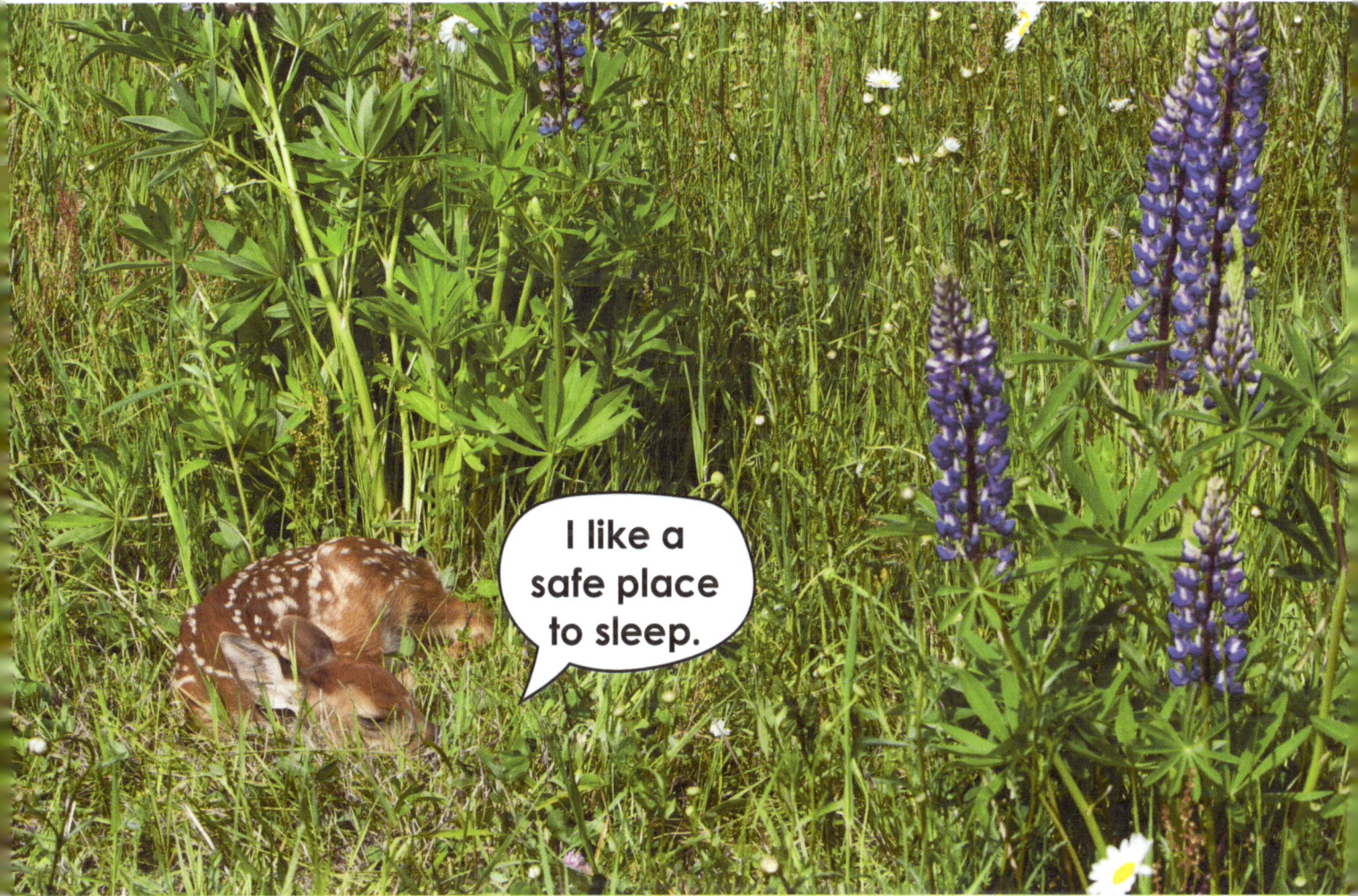

They also sleep in the shelter of shrubs and thickets.

Deer are most active during the dawn and dusk.

I enjoy the sunrise and sunset.

I do not sleep all night but take short naps during the day and night.

Some animals like wolves, cougars, and coyotes might try to catch deer.

Deer are good at hiding, jumping, and running fast to escape predators.

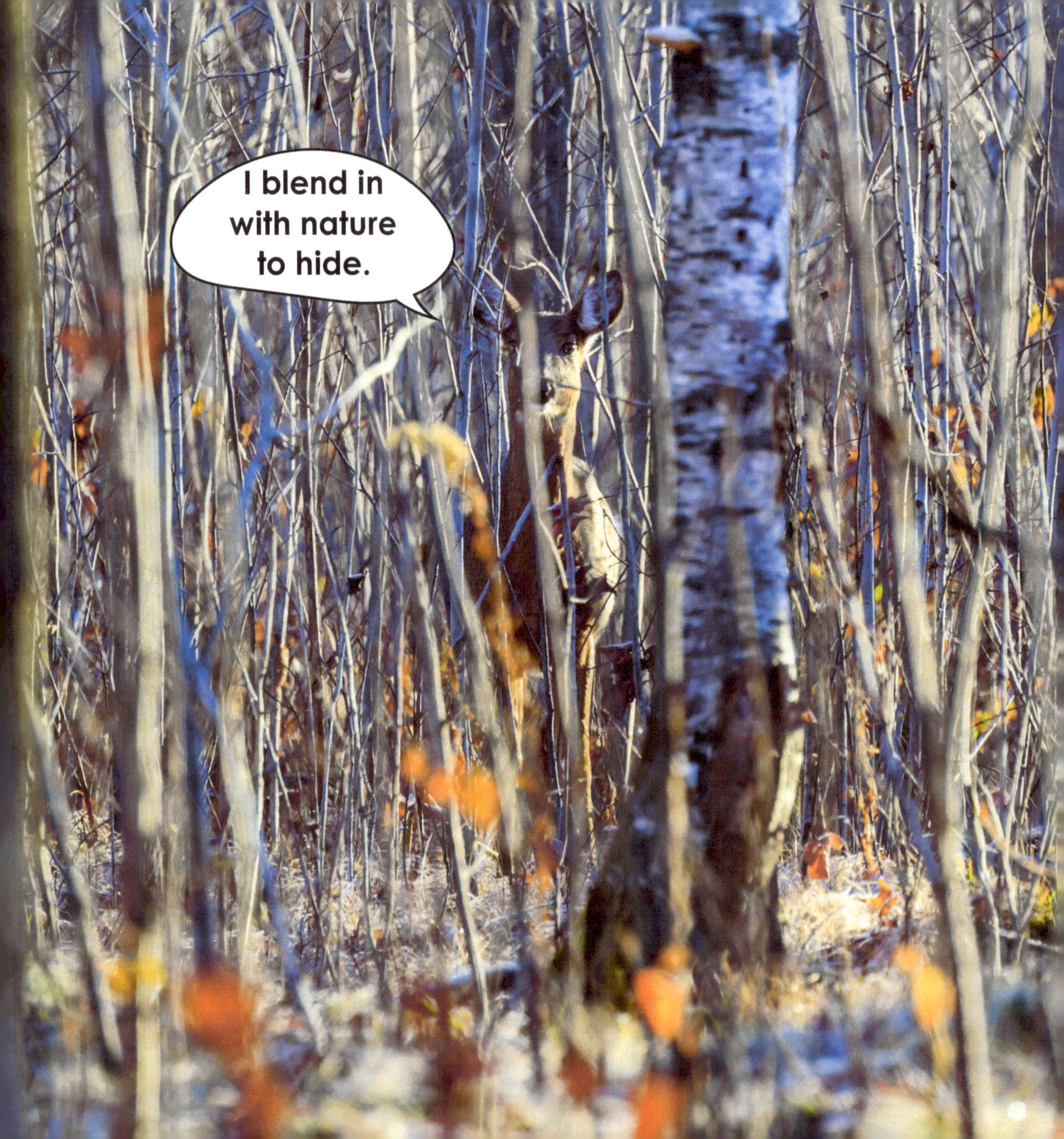
I blend in with nature to hide.

Many deer can run at speeds of 30 to 35 miles per hour (48 to 56 km) for short distances.

Deer can paddle through the water.

Deer can be 2 to 3.5 feet (1m) tall at their shoulders.

Deer have big ears that help them hear sounds far away.

Deer have big, round eyes that help them see well in the dark.

The most common deer are white-tailed deer and mule deer.

Deer are vegetarians!

Deer eat plants like leaves, grass, and flowers.

Baby deer are called "fawns".

Some fawns have spots
when they're young.

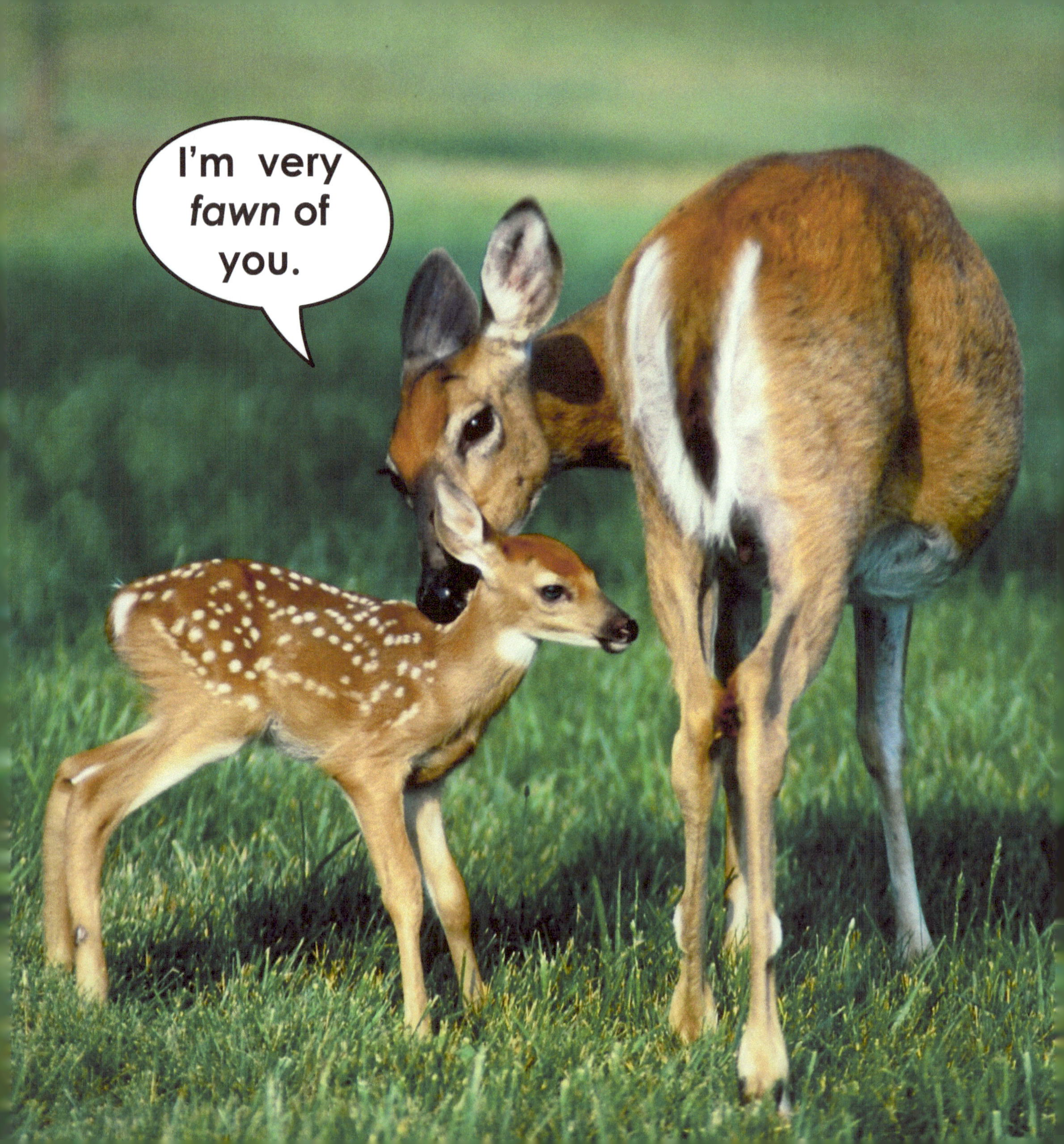
I'm very *fawn* of you.

Fawns stay close to their mom for 6 to 8 months.

Sometimes deer move to find food or a better home, especially in cold winters.

Deer can be very gentle with their deer friends and family.

Deer often spend time with other deer in a group called a "herd".

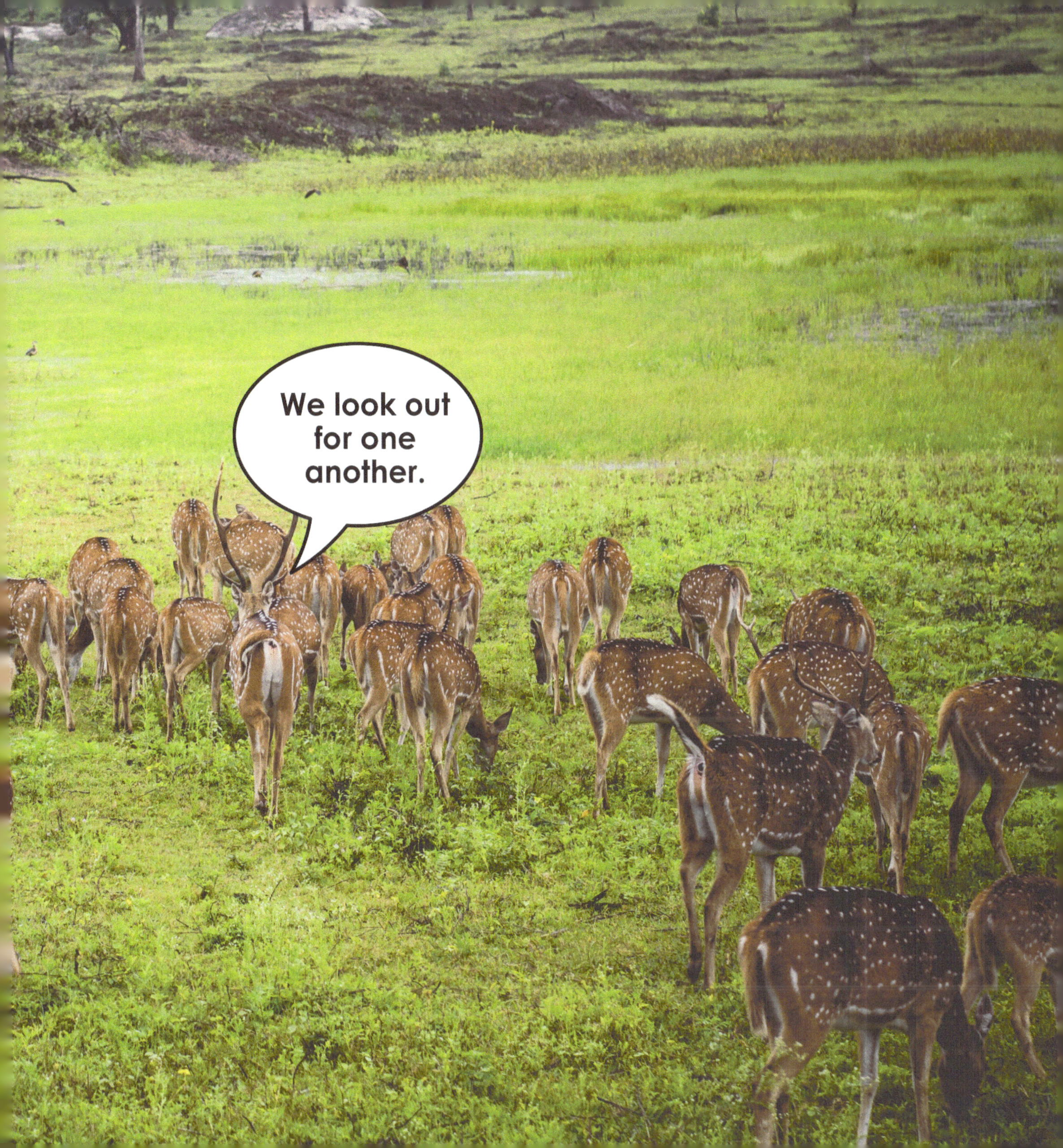
We look out for one another.

Deer talk to each other with sounds like soft calls.

Hey! What's up?

They also stomp their hooves to alert other deer.

Deer can live for about 10 to 15 years in the wild.

People like to watch deer, but it's important to be quiet and not disturb them.

Want more?

... and more

Hello parents!

Visit us to find out about new releases and **FREE** offers. We'll let you know when we have a new release coming out and how you can get it for FREE.

And you can cast your vote for what book we make next!

scan here

ActiveBrainsBooks.com

or visit here

---

scan here

Let us know what you think. As an independent publisher, your honest reviews mean a lot to us and our business. We'd love to hear from you!

amazon.com/review/create-review/

or visit here

FOLLOW US on Amazon.

amazon.com/author/activebrainsbooks

ActiveBrainsBooks.com

ACTIVE BRAINS

www.ingramcontent.com/pod-product-compliance
Lightning Source LLC
Chambersburg PA
CBHW060844270326
41933CB00003B/188